Unicorn Magic World : Fun and Relaxing Coloring book: for Kids

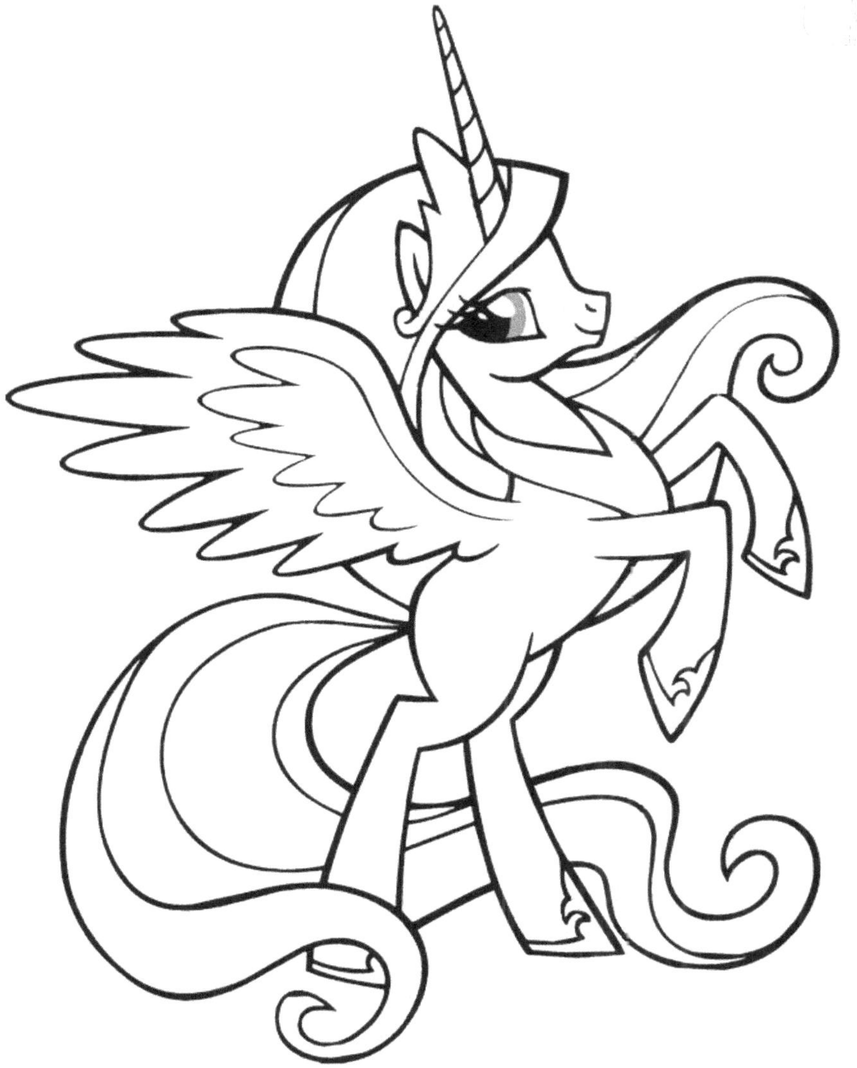

Nina Packer

Unicorn Magic World Coloring book For Kids

Copyright: Published in the United States by Nina packer
Published February 2018

ISBN-13: 978-1985899629

ISBN-10: 1985899620

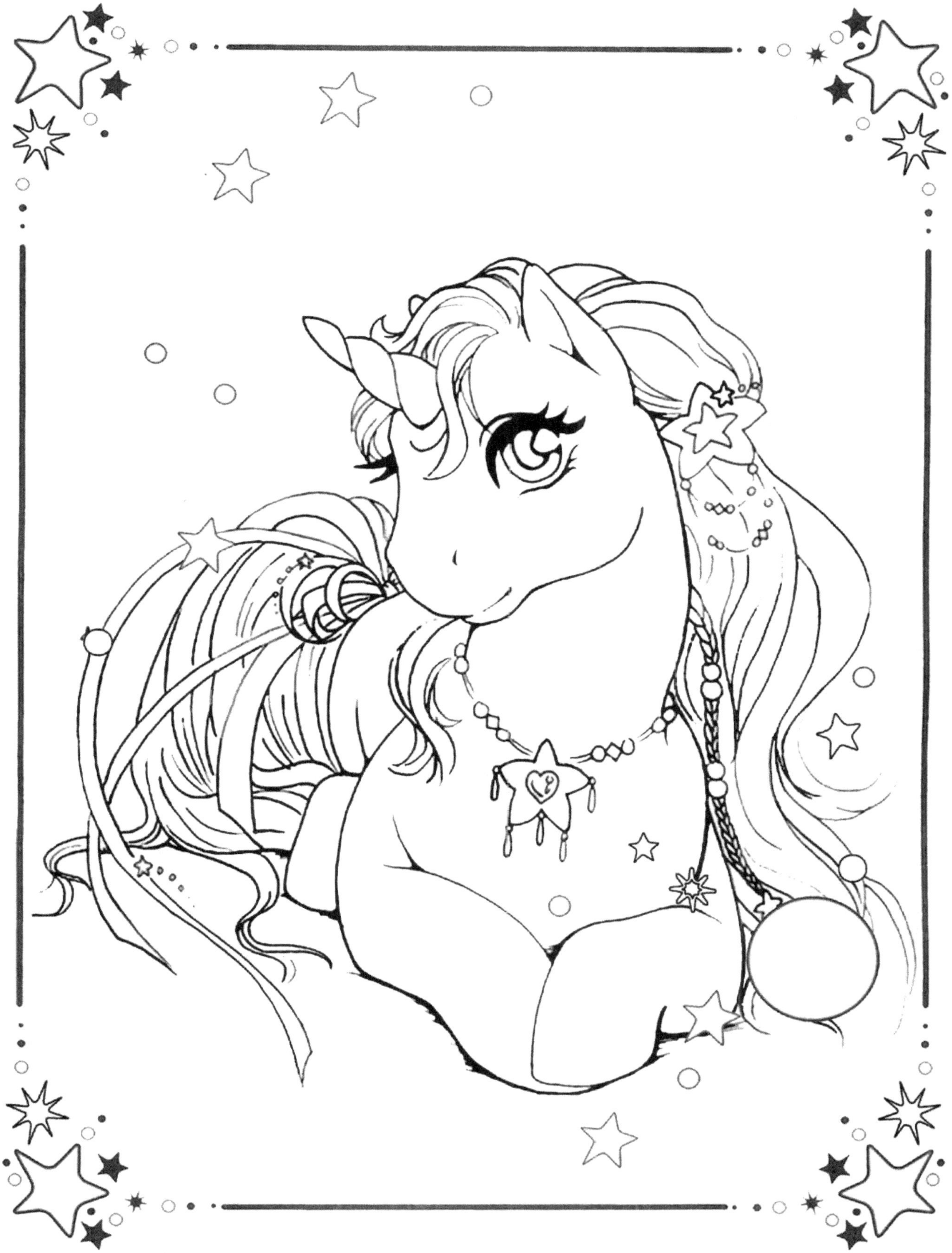

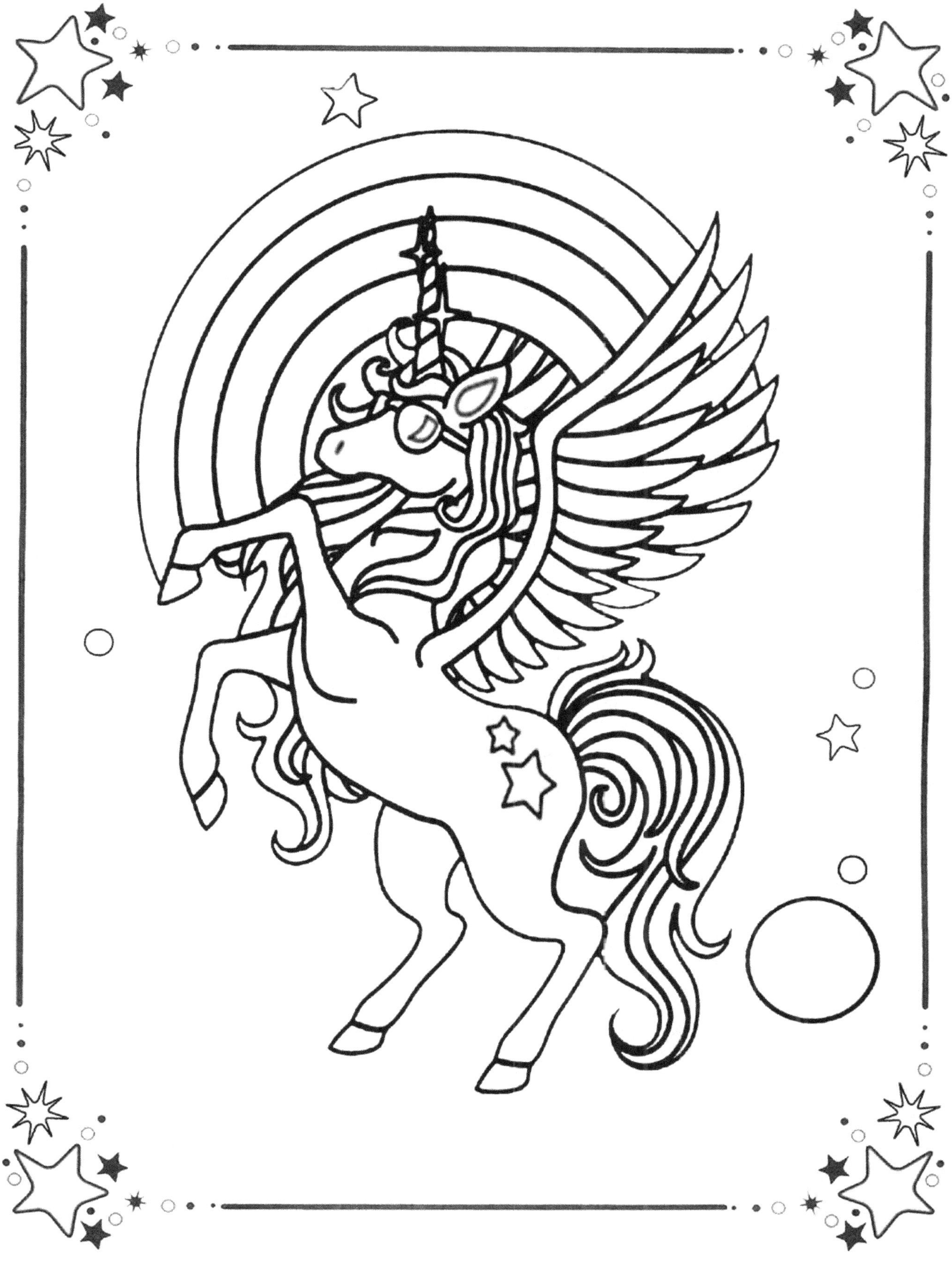

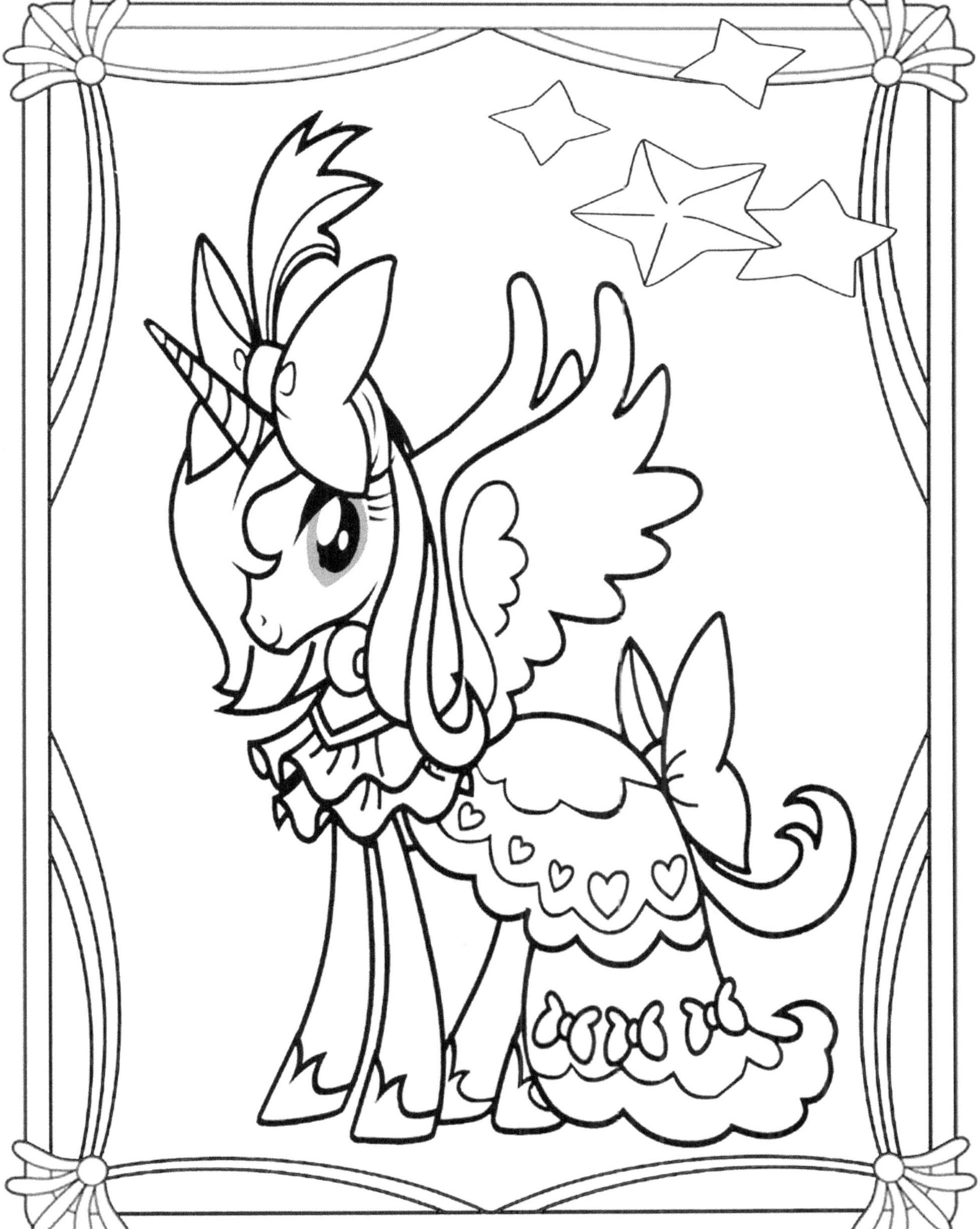

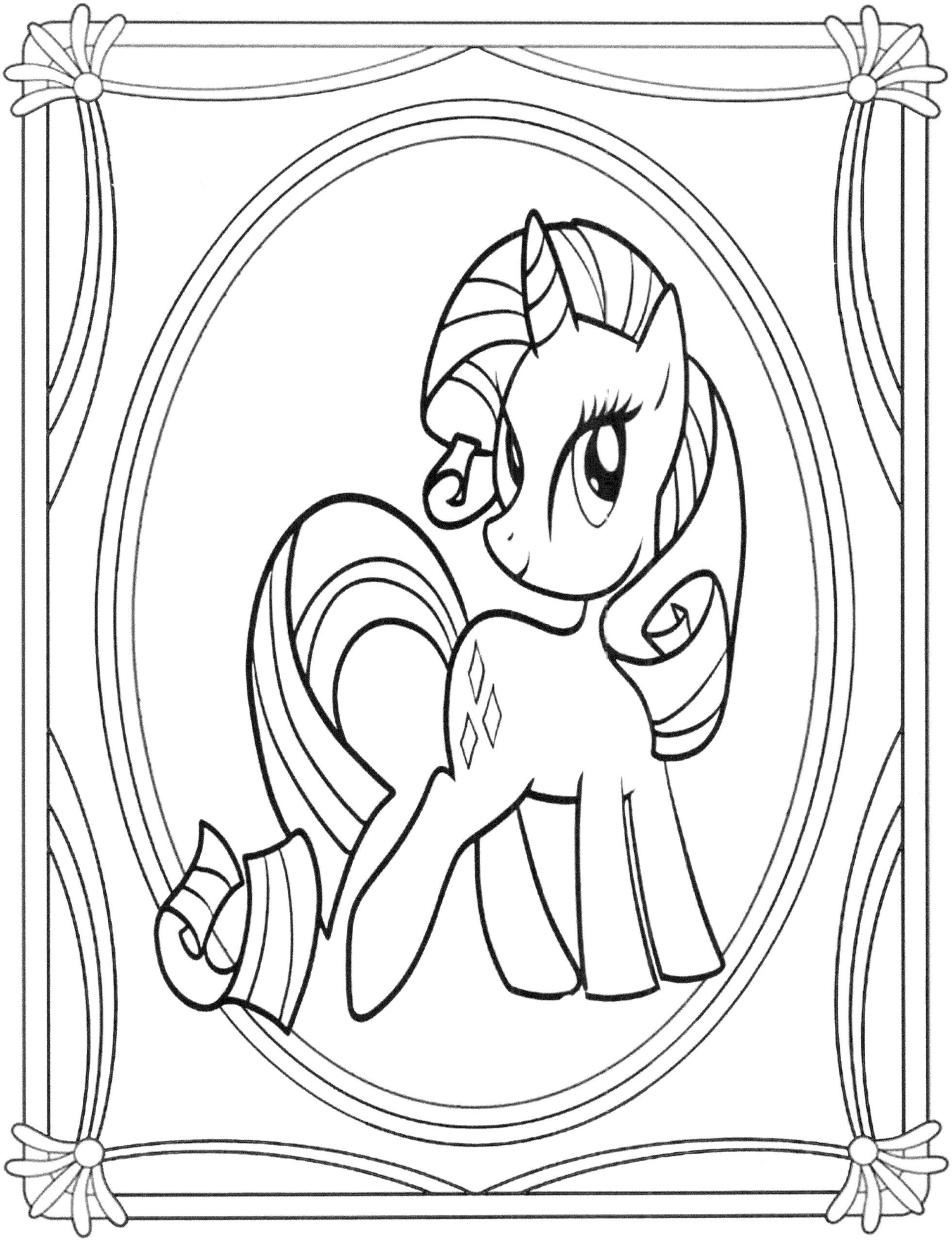

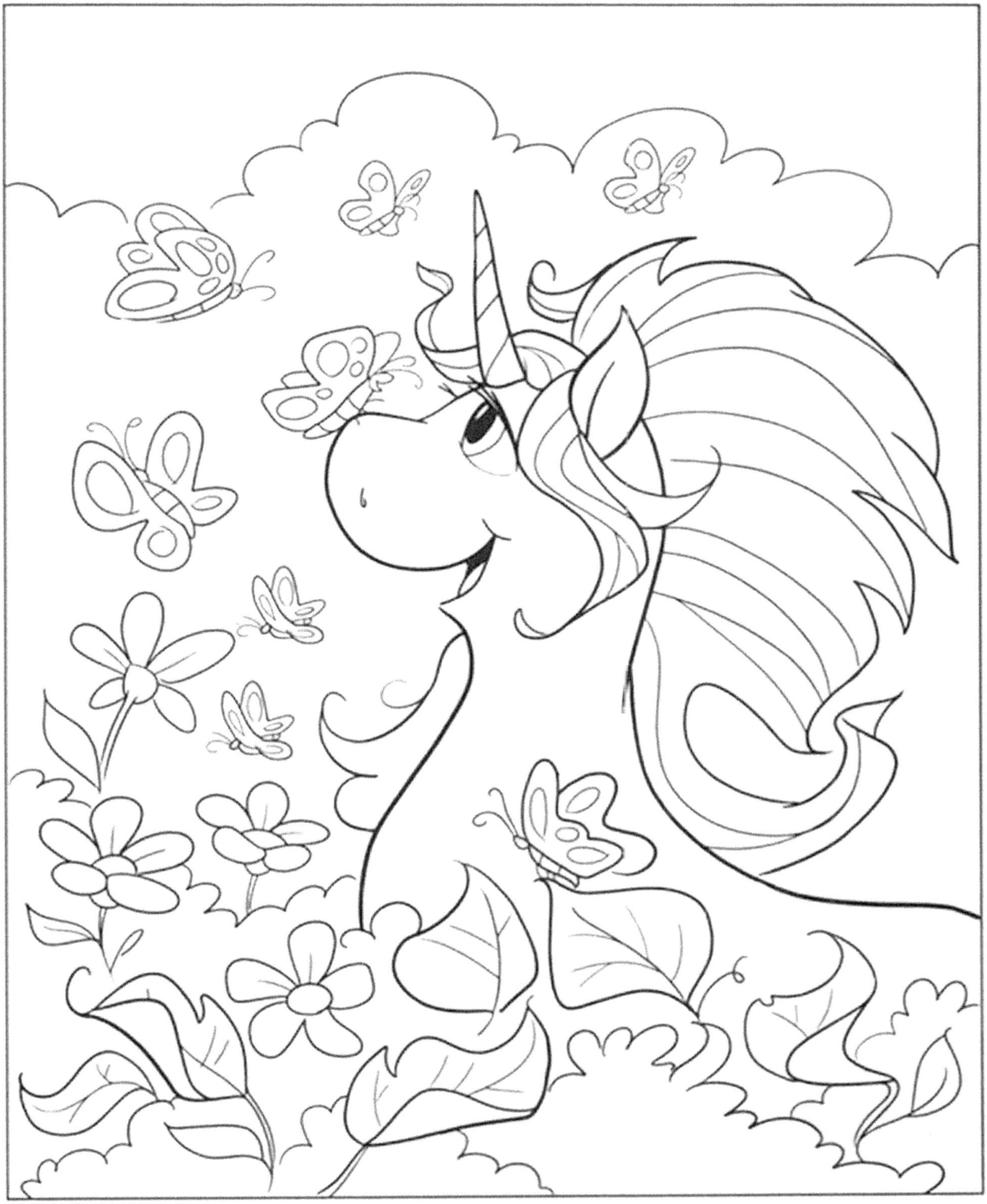

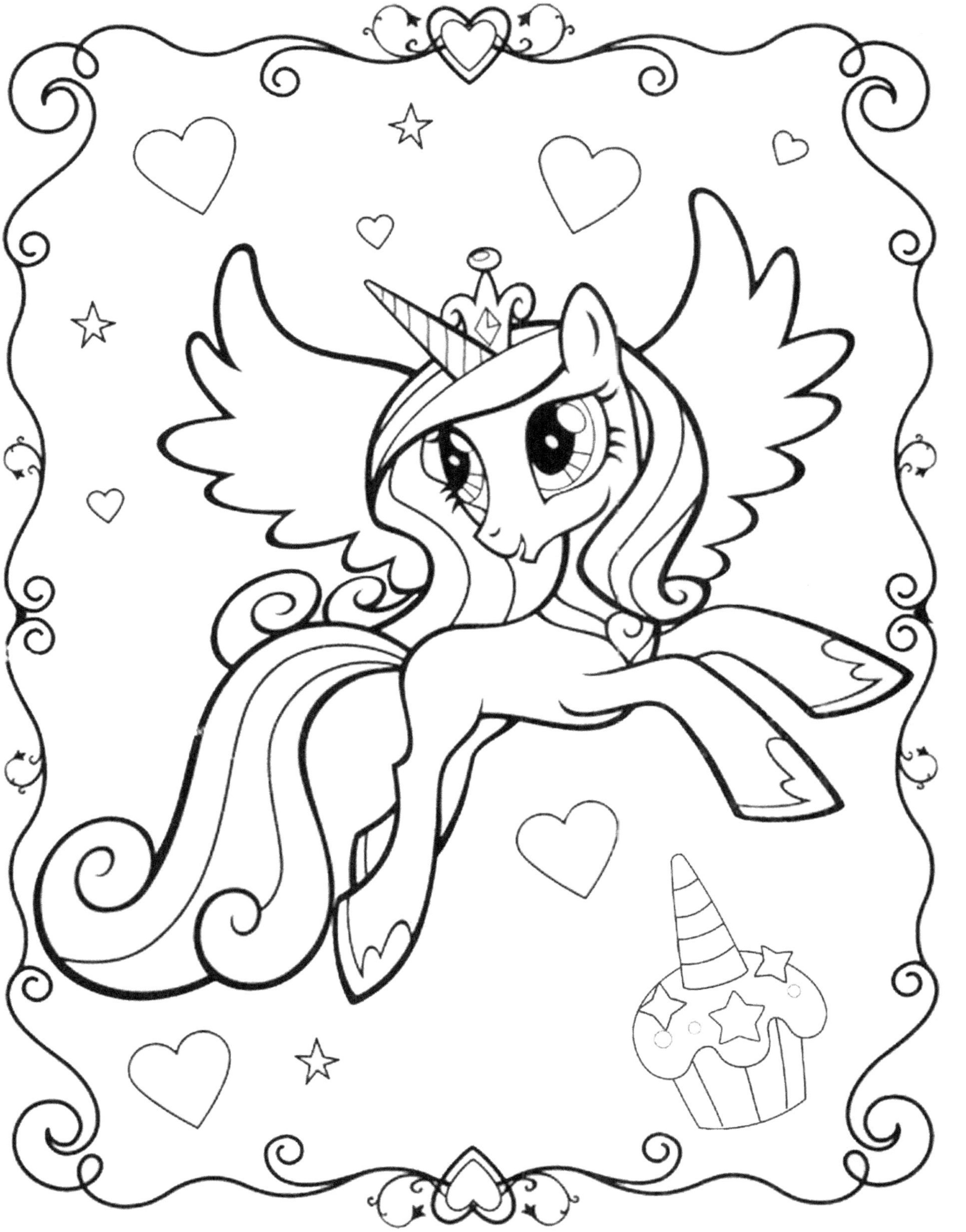

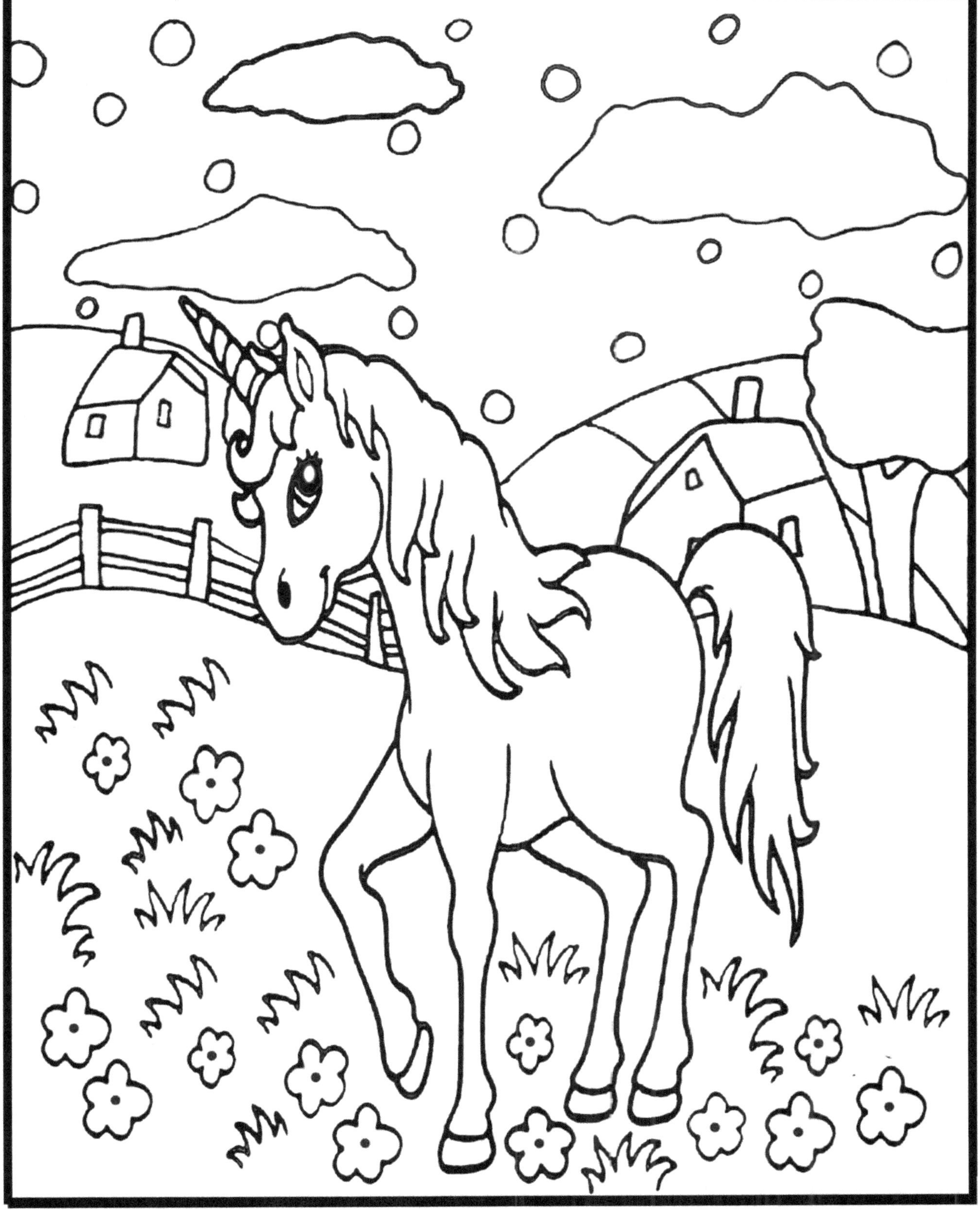

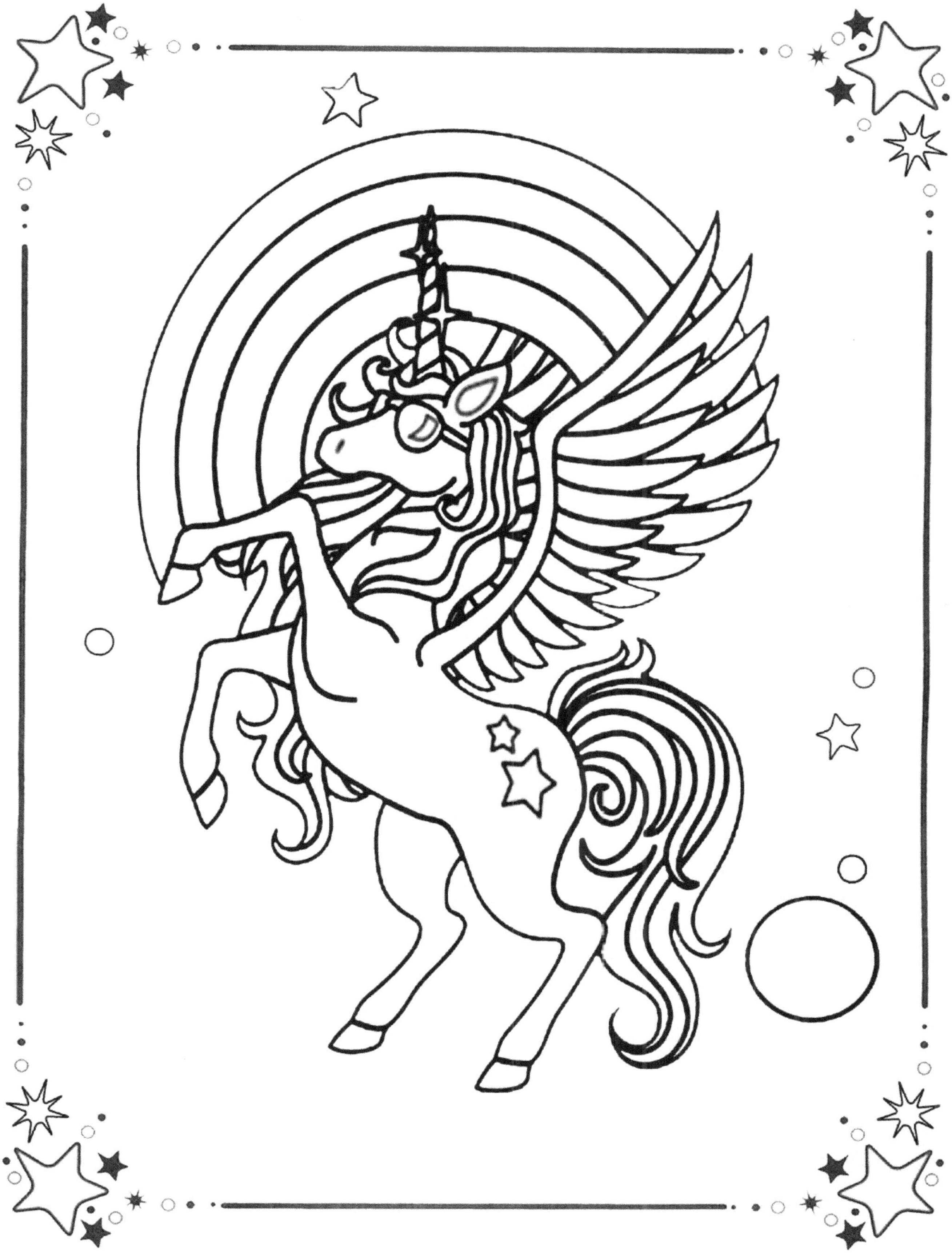

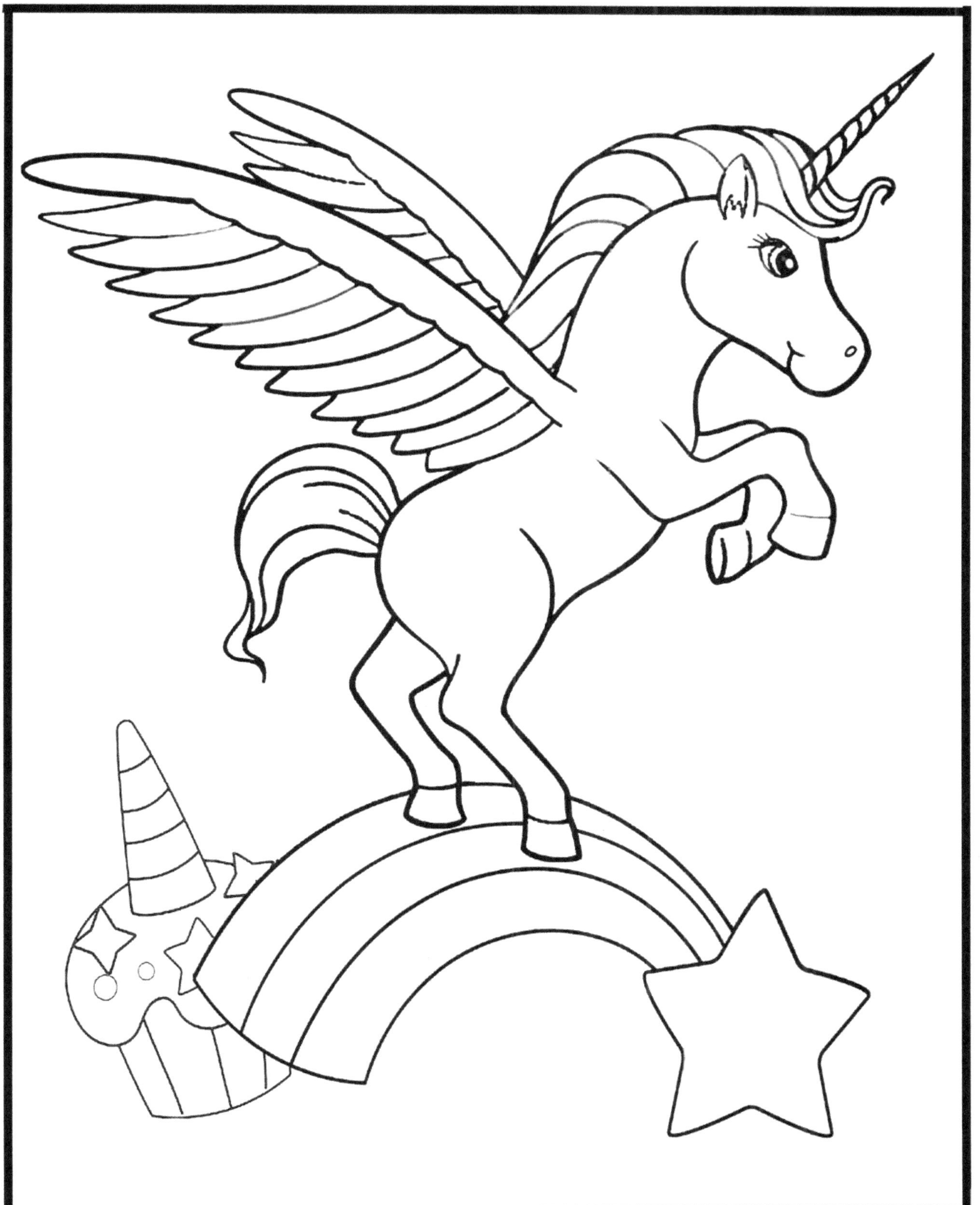

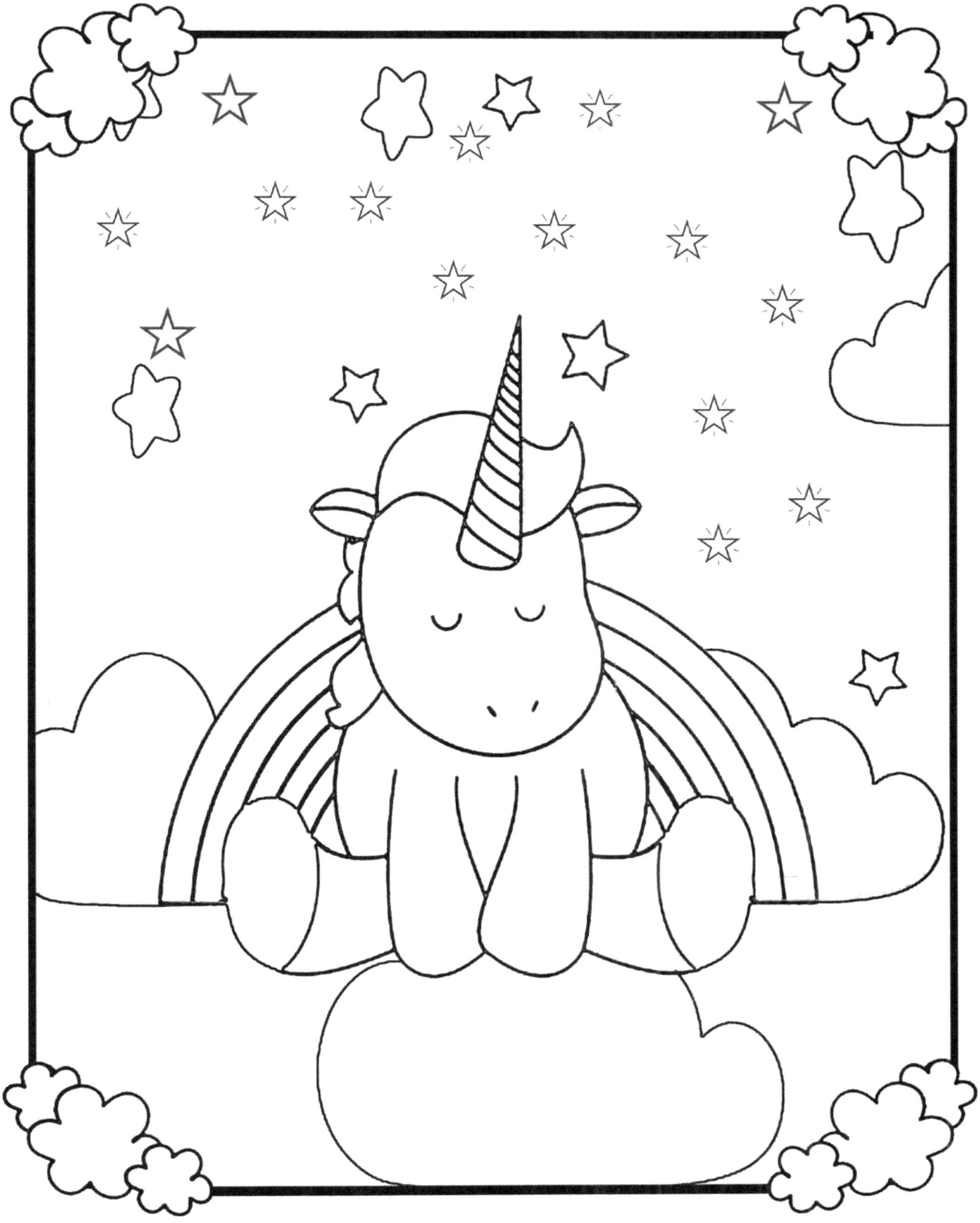

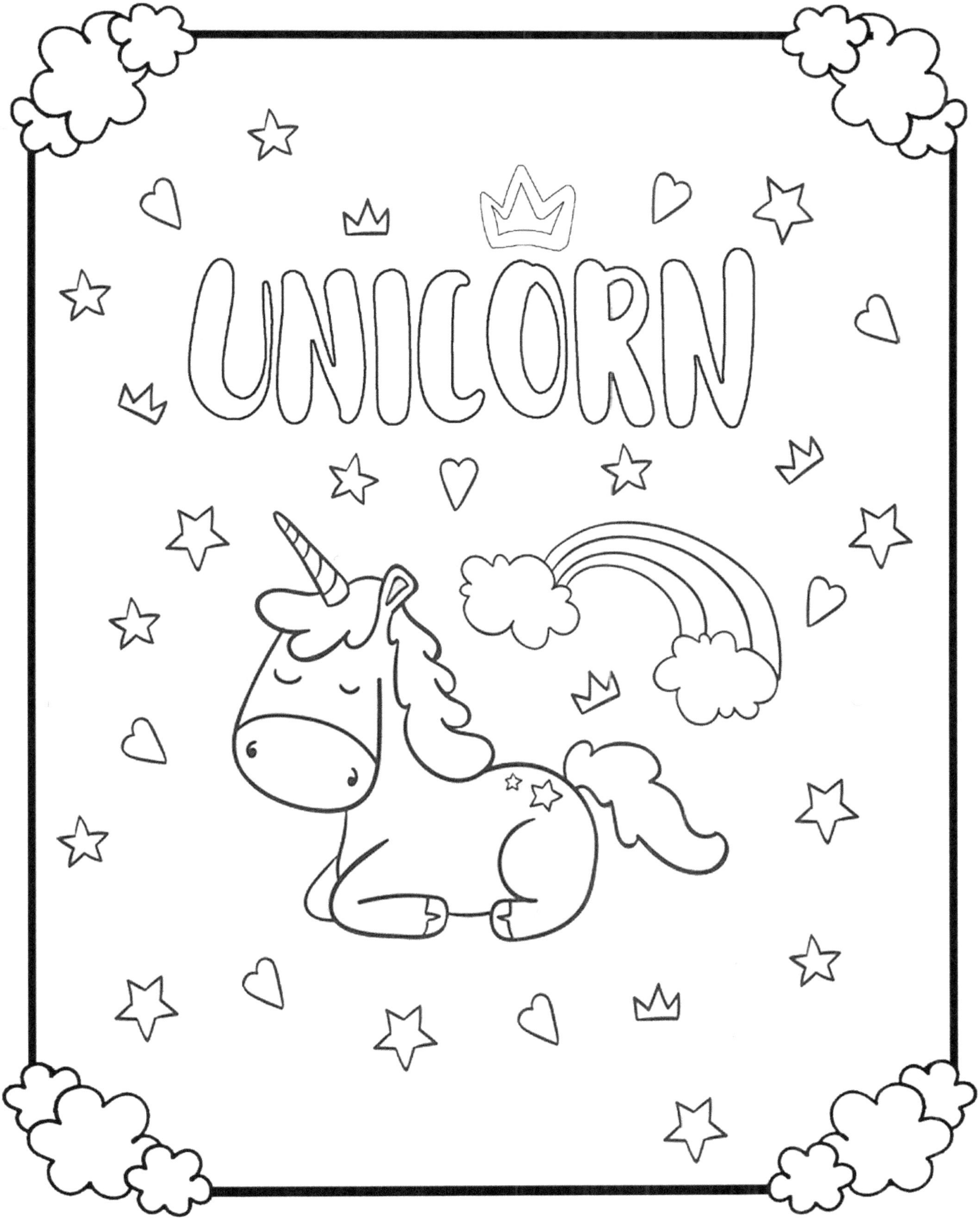
UNICORN

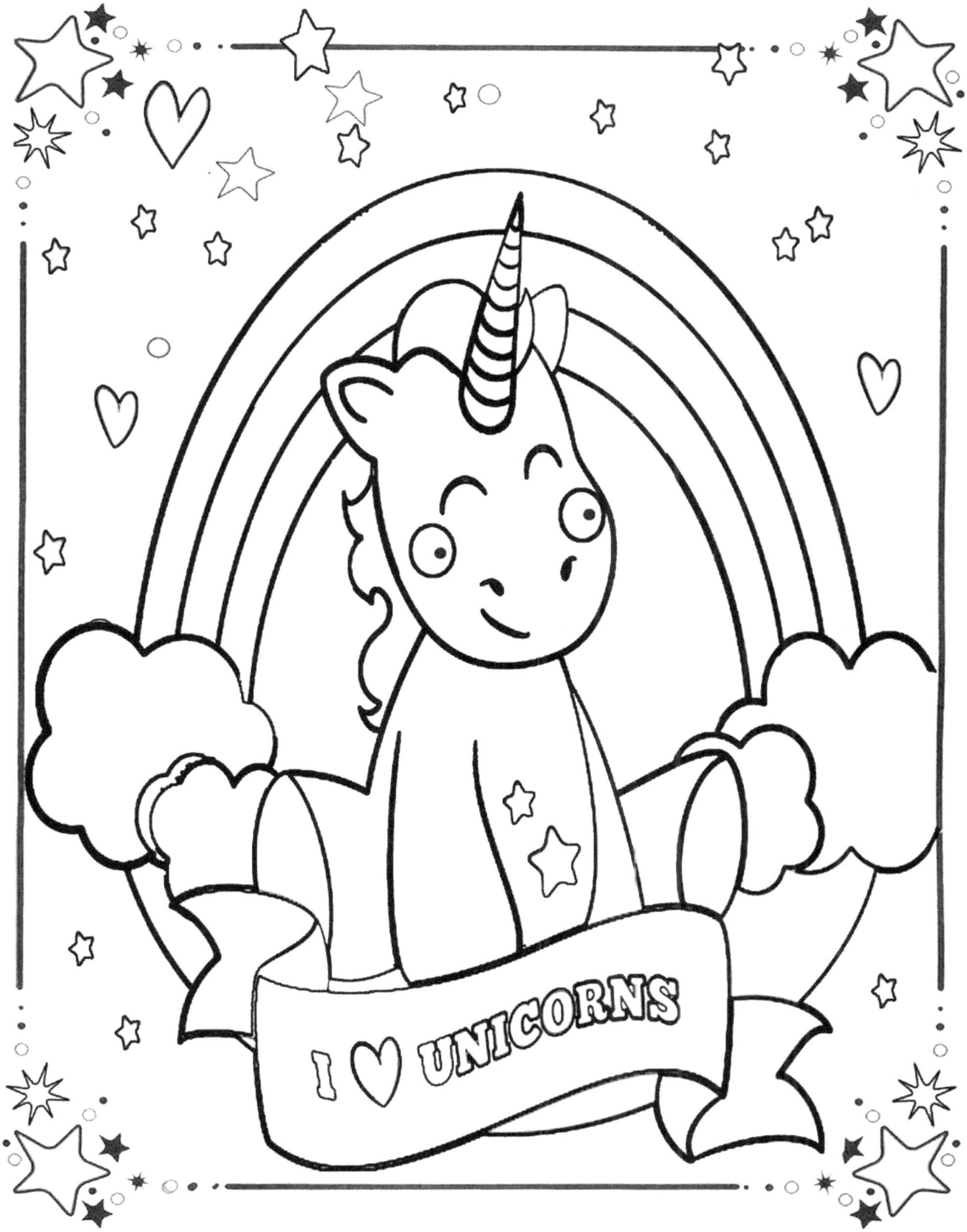
I ♥ UNICORNS

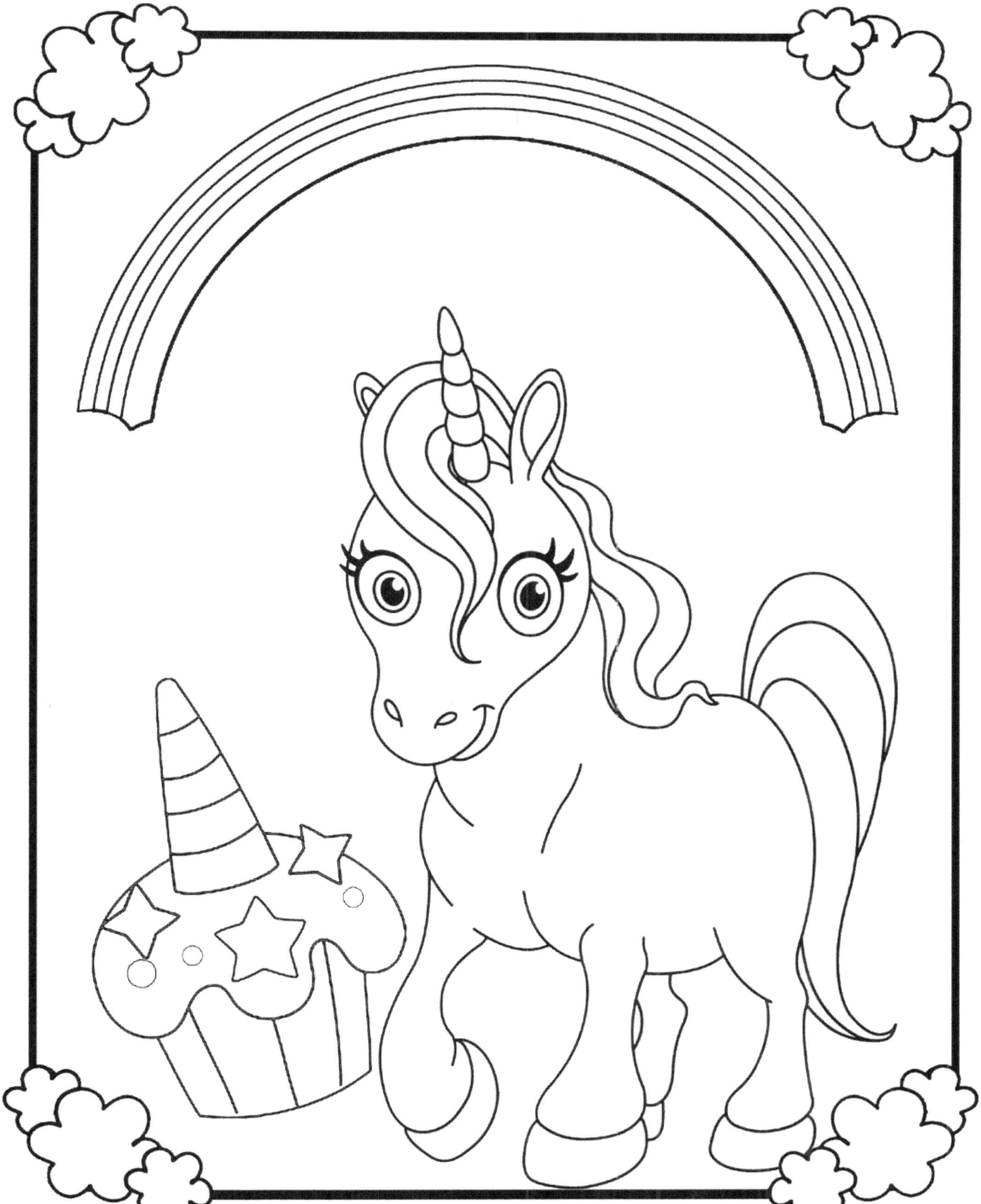

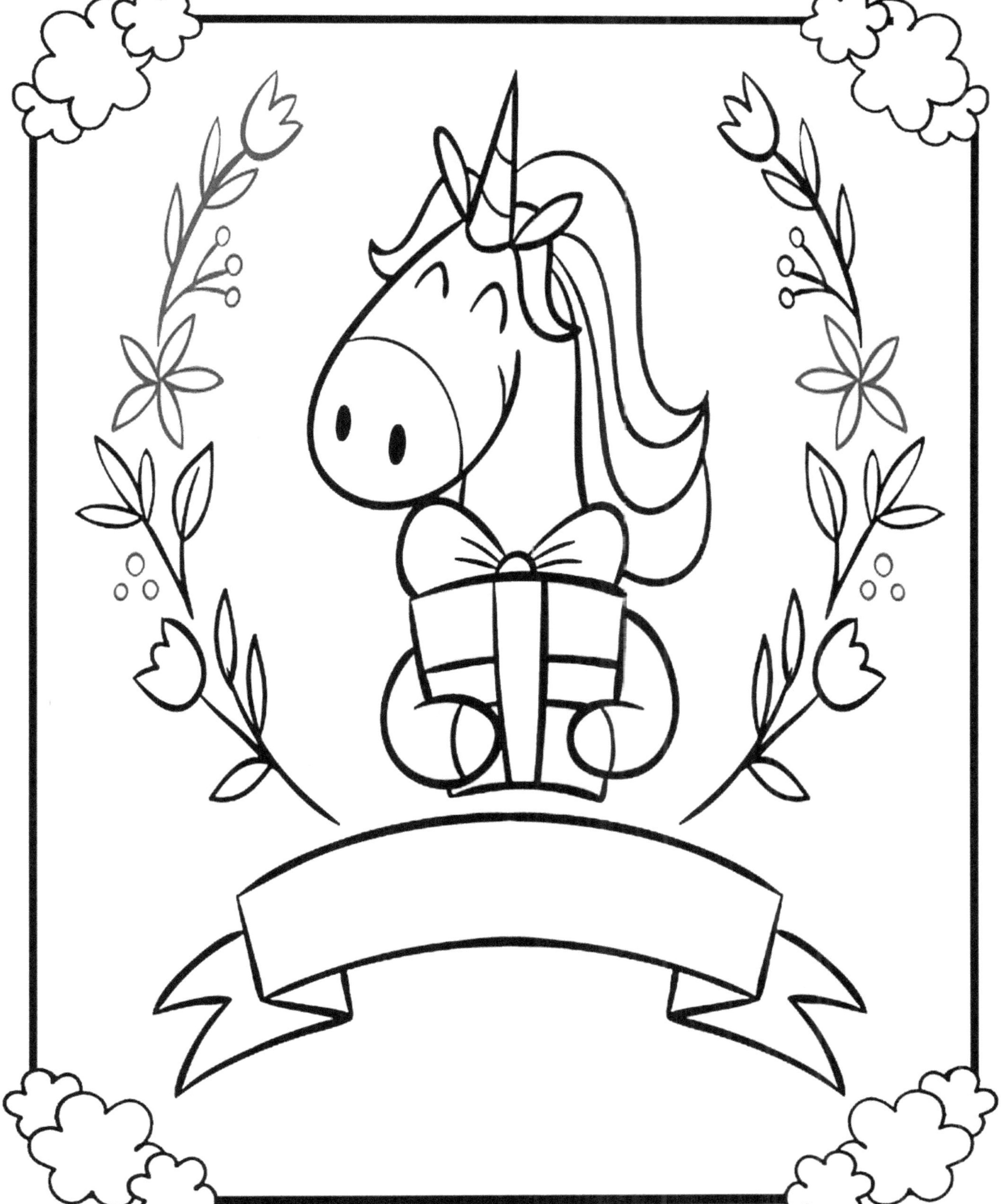

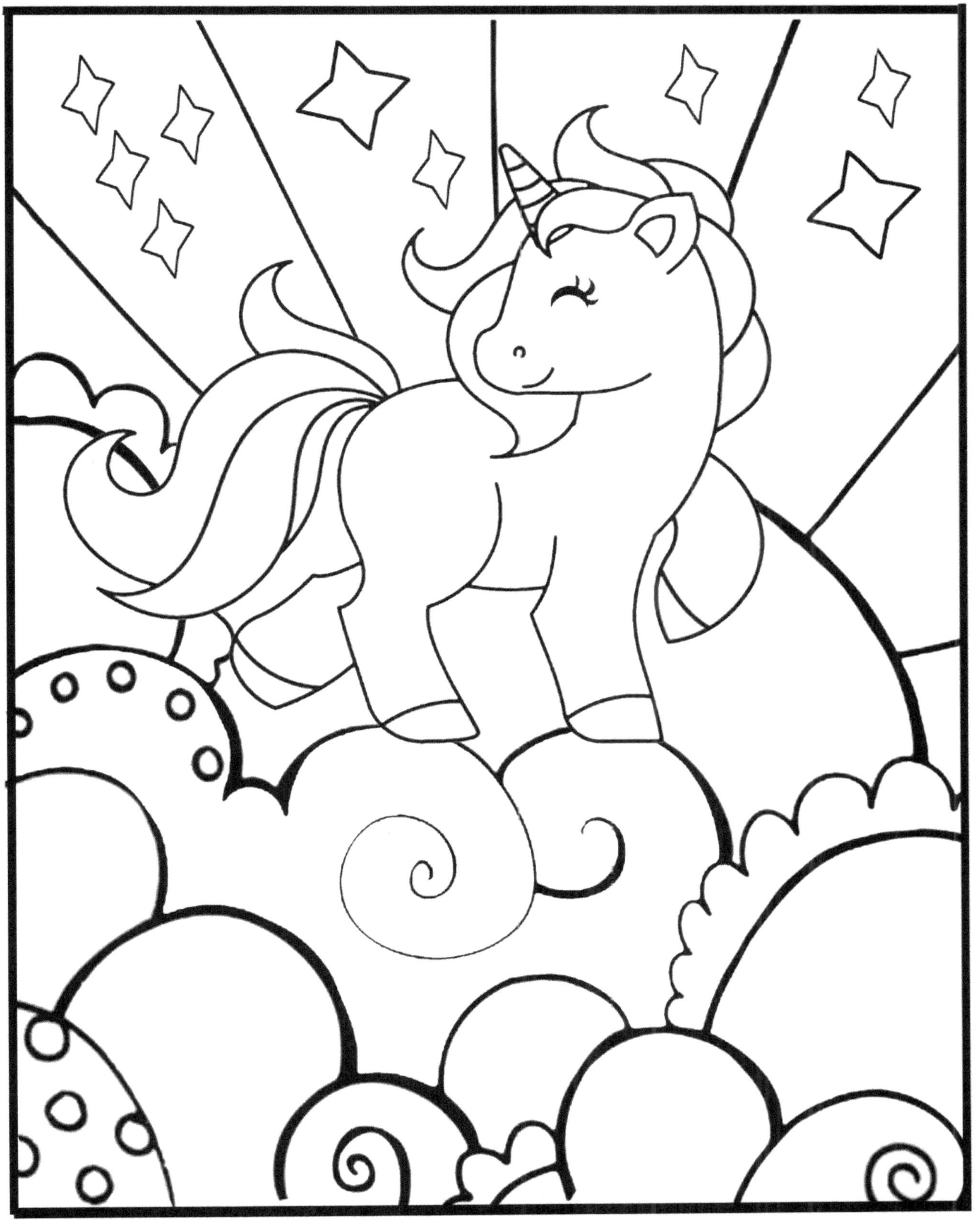

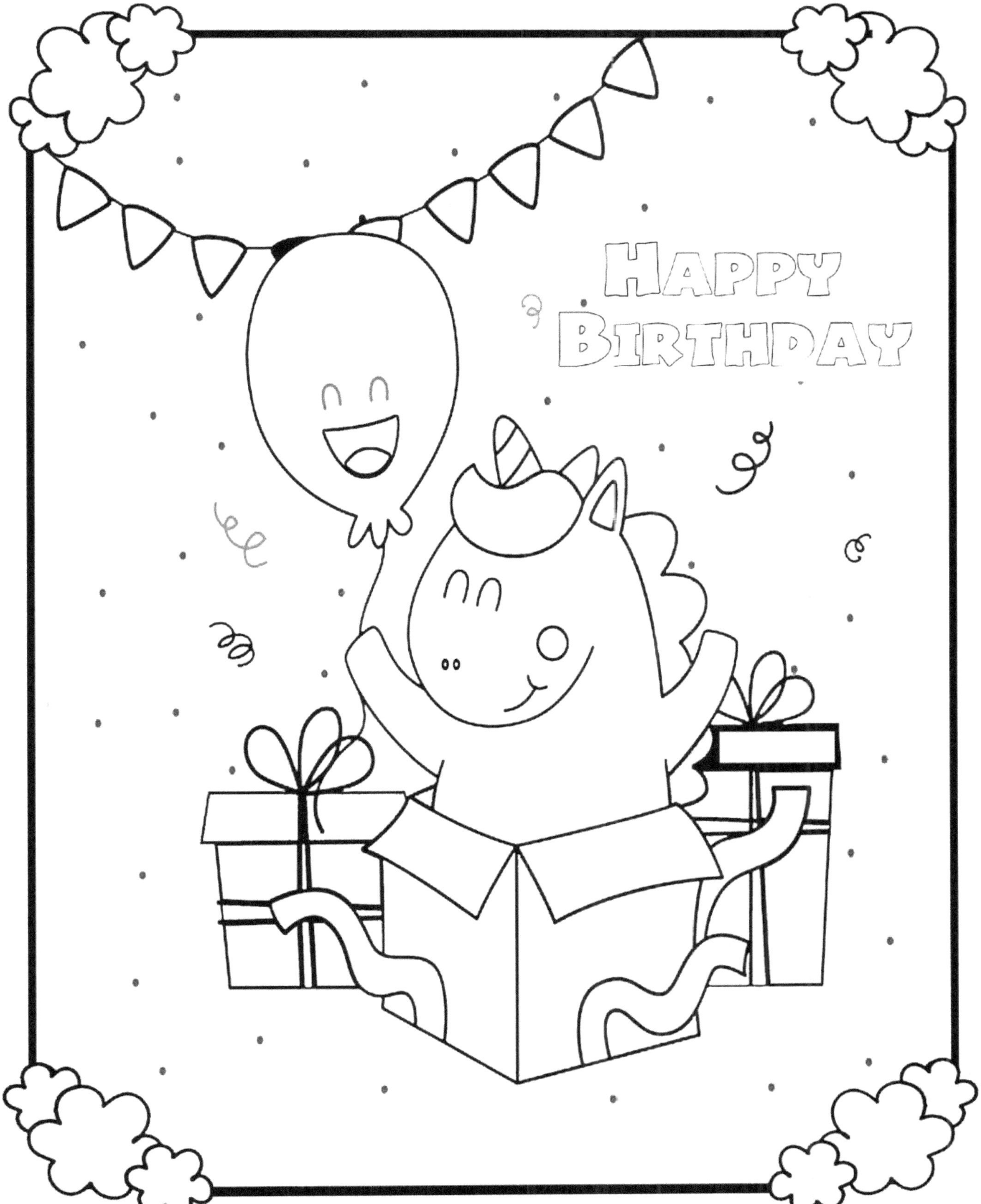
HAPPY
BIRTHDAY

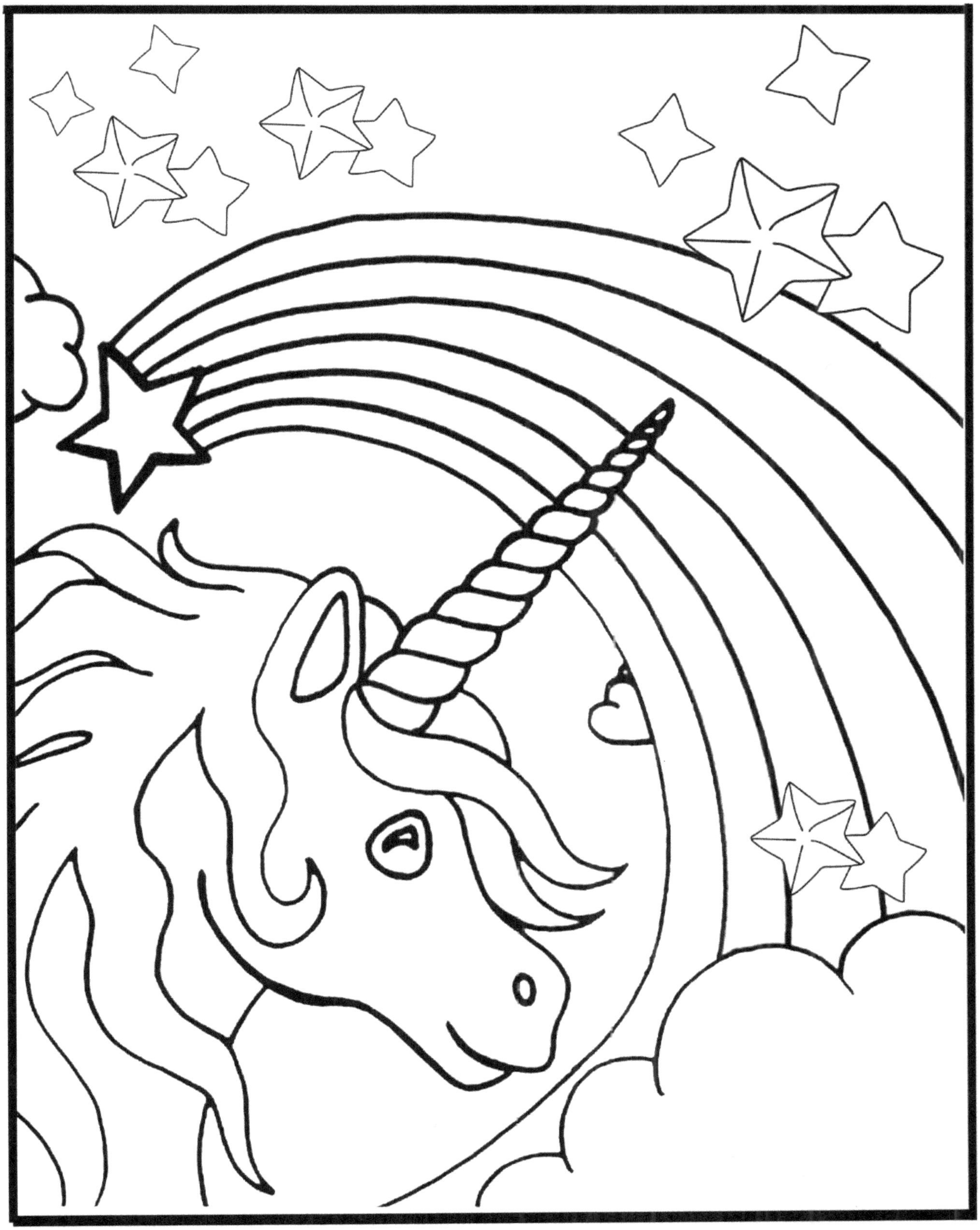

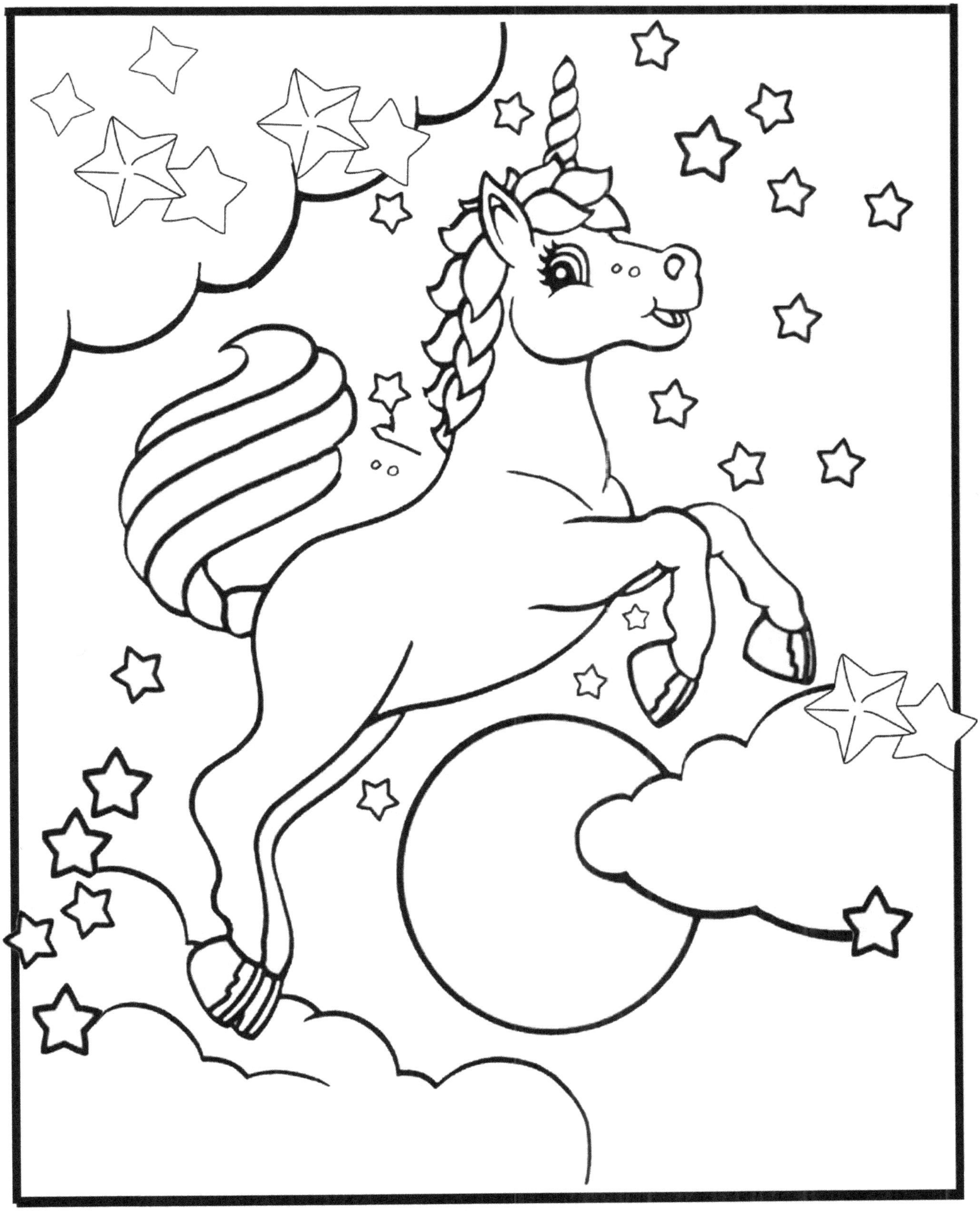

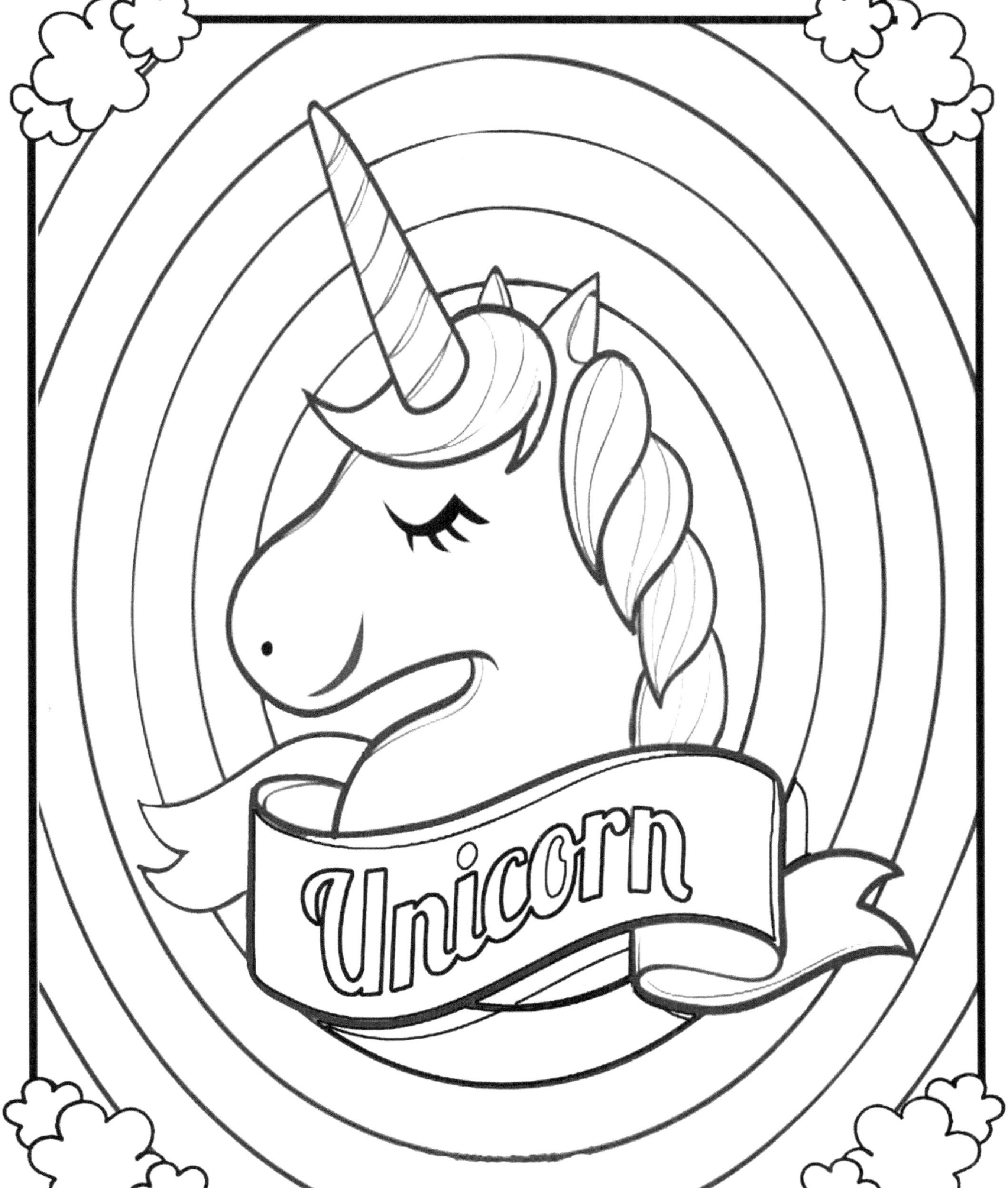
Unicorn

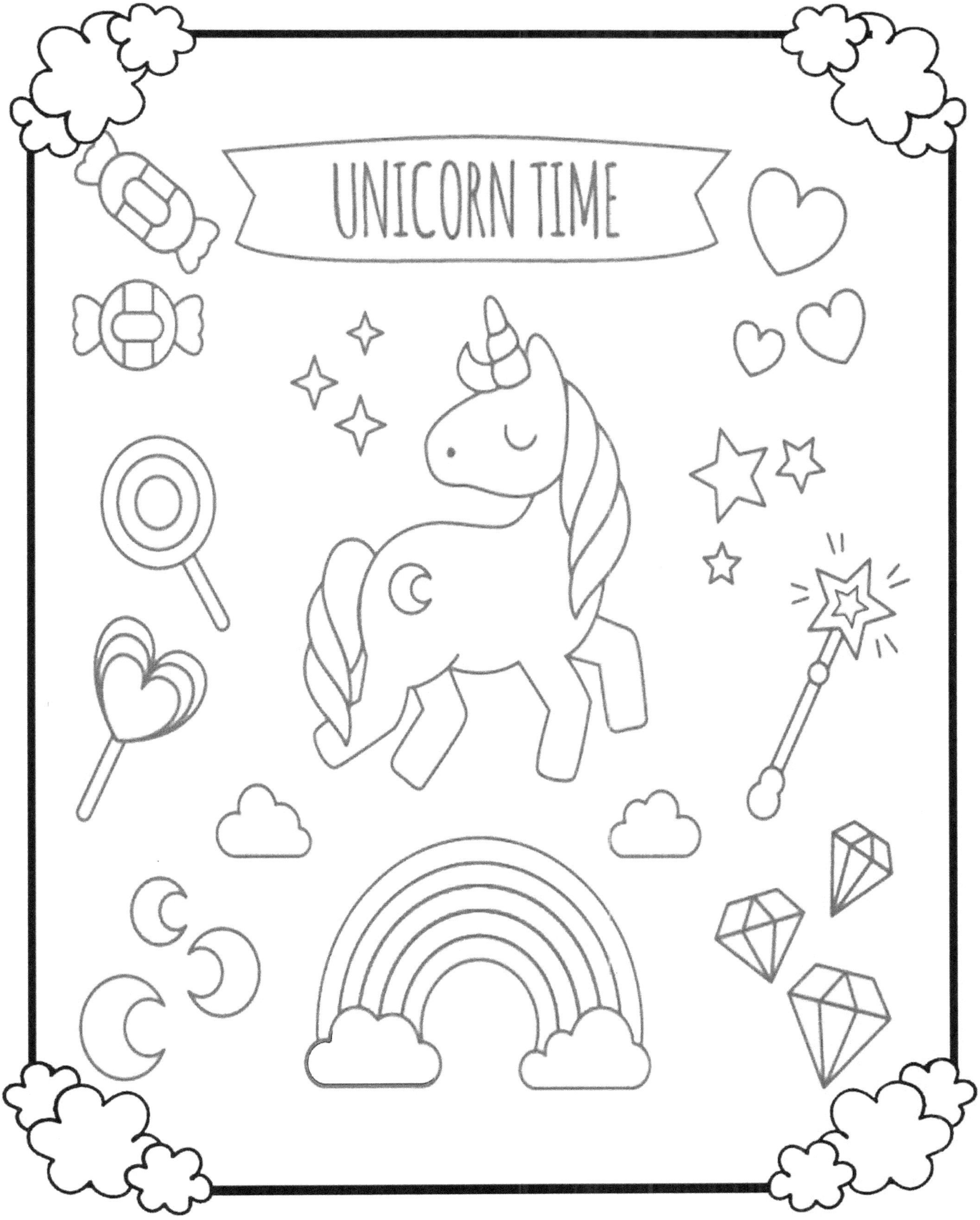
UNICORN TIME

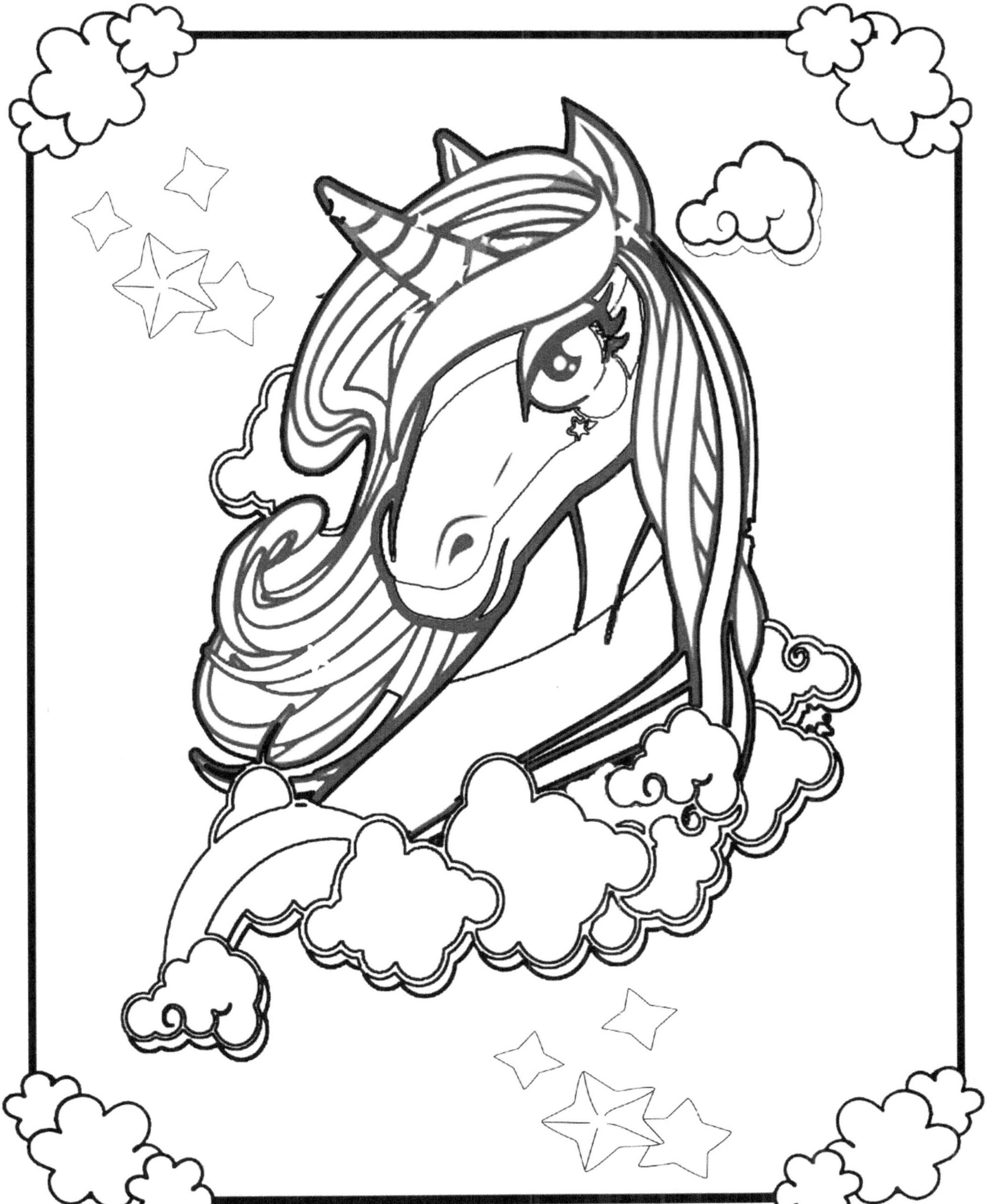

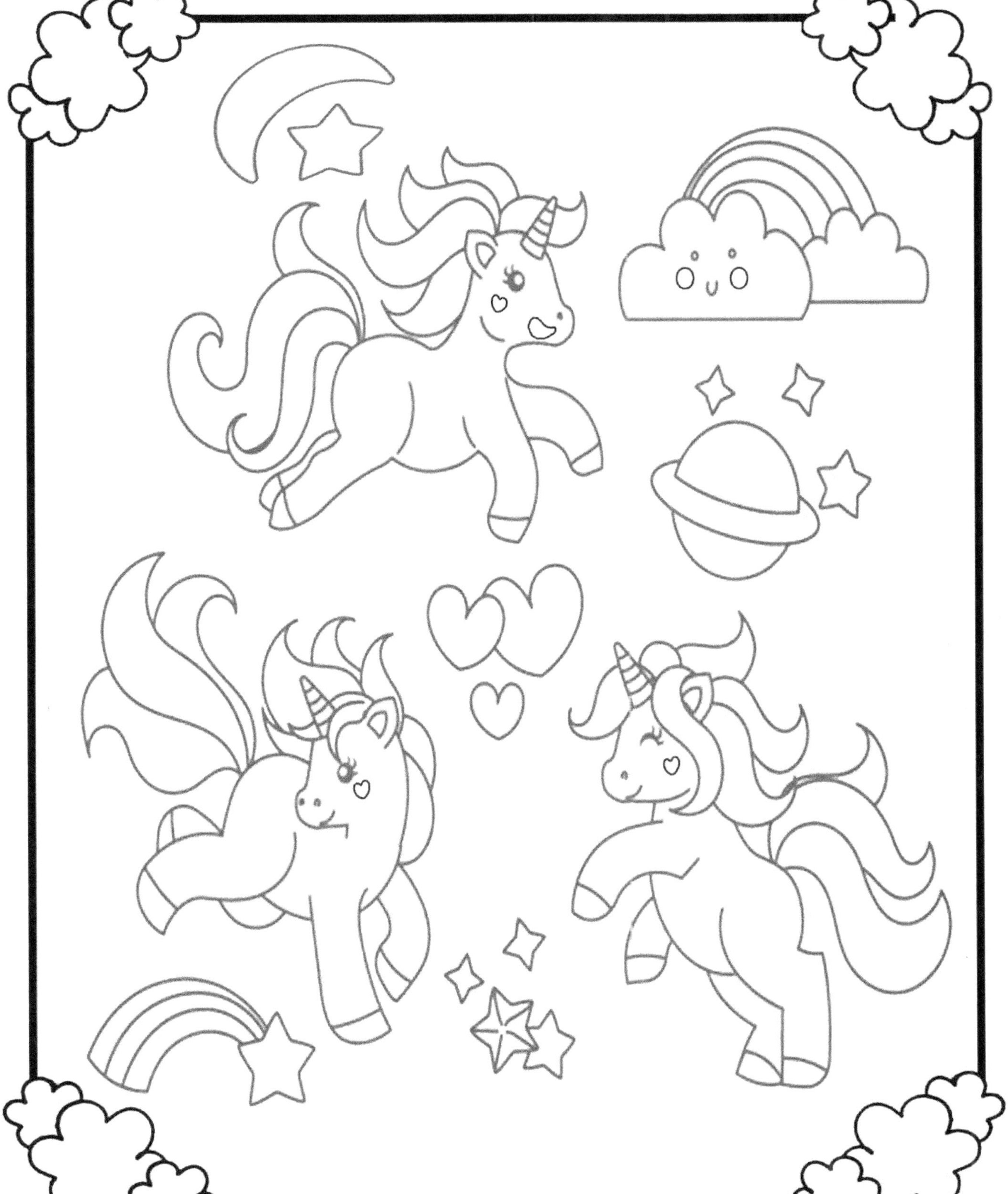

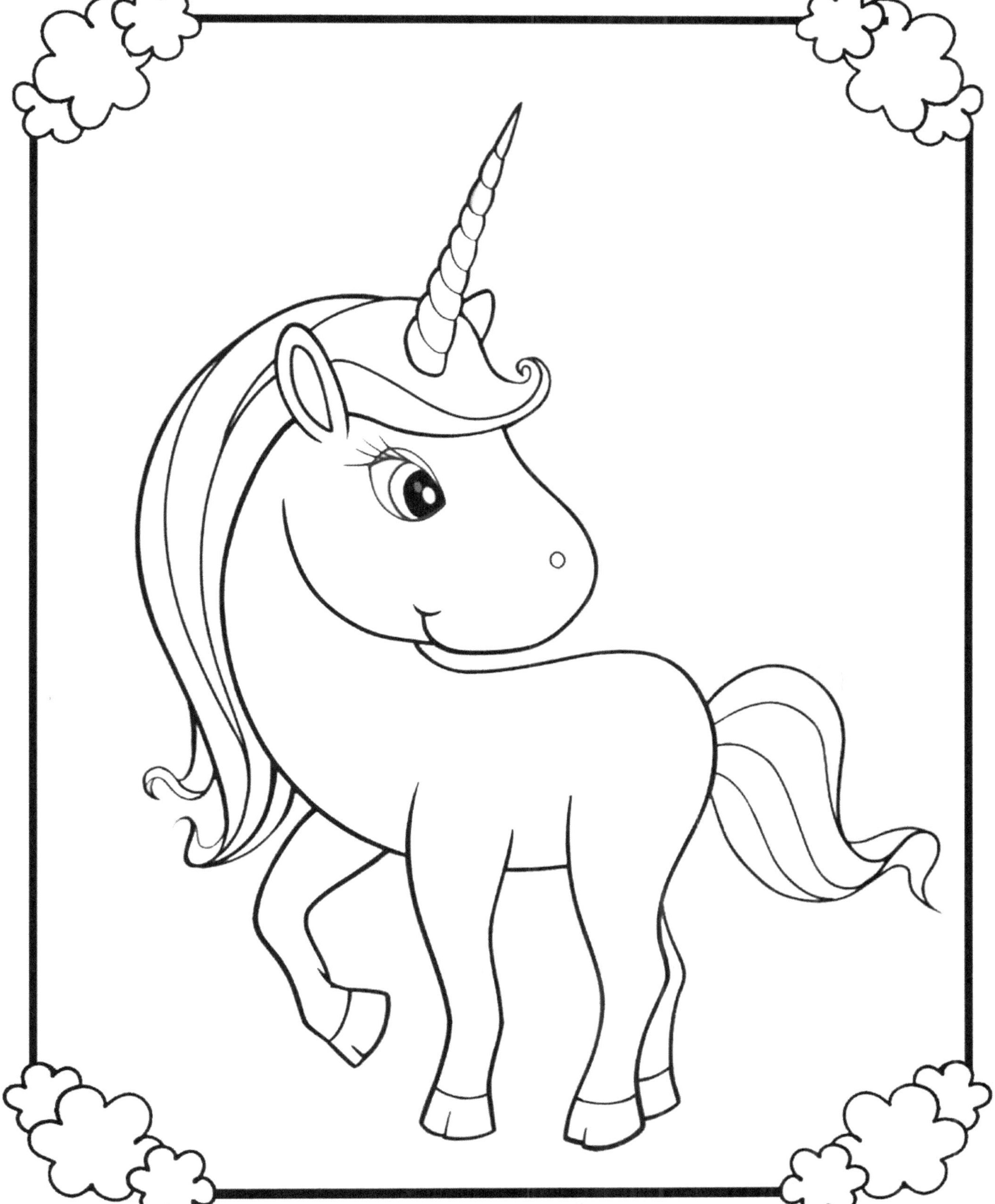

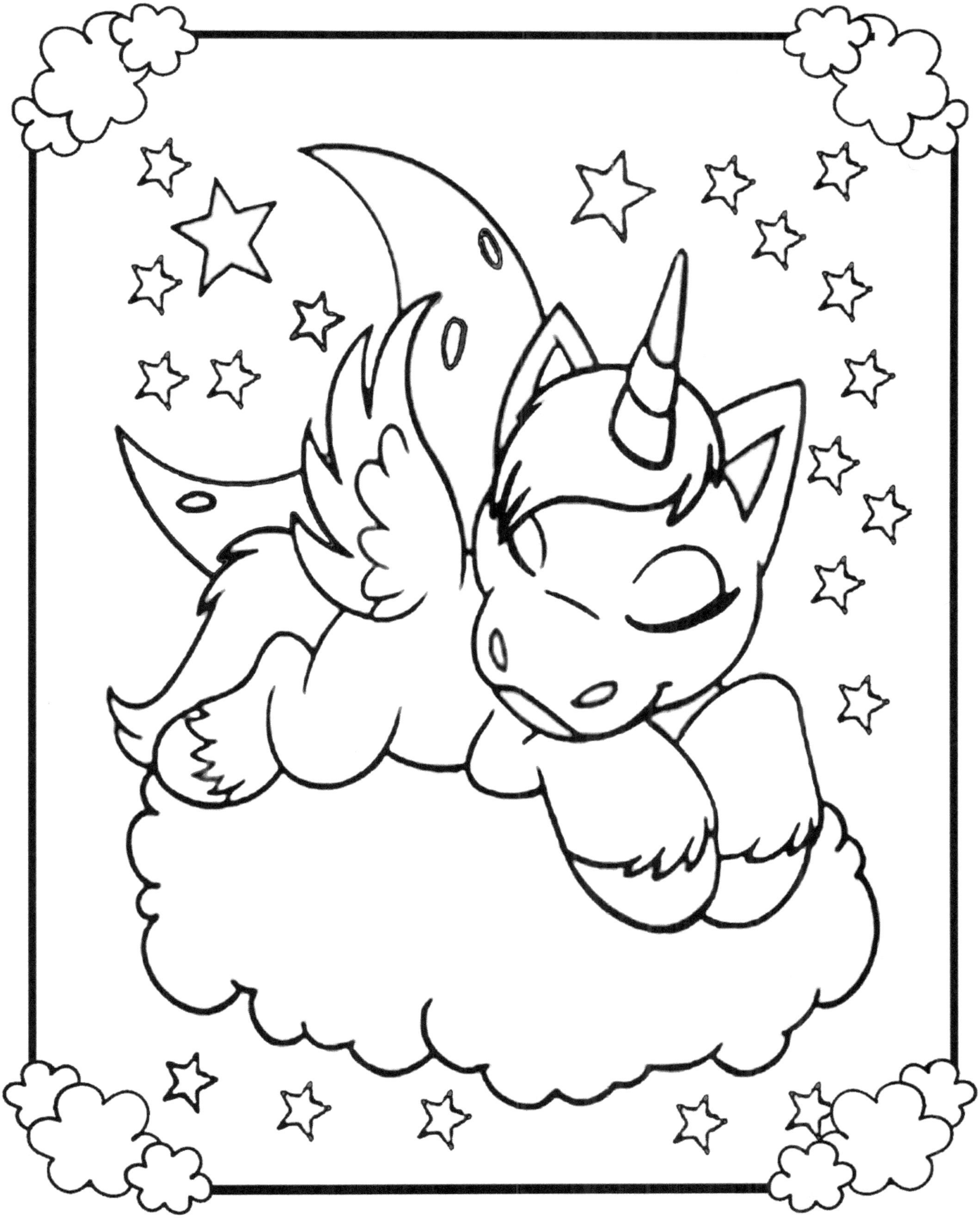

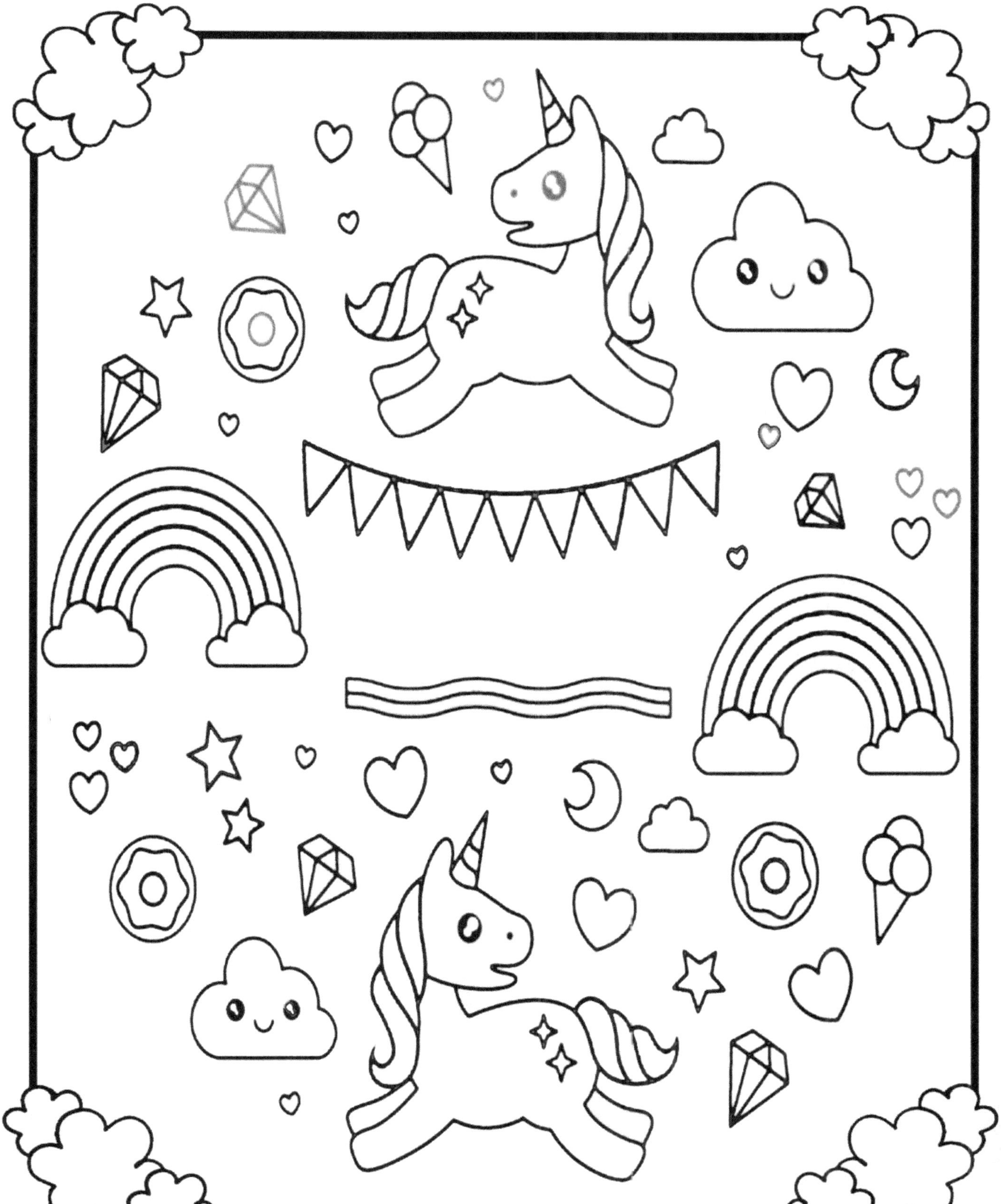

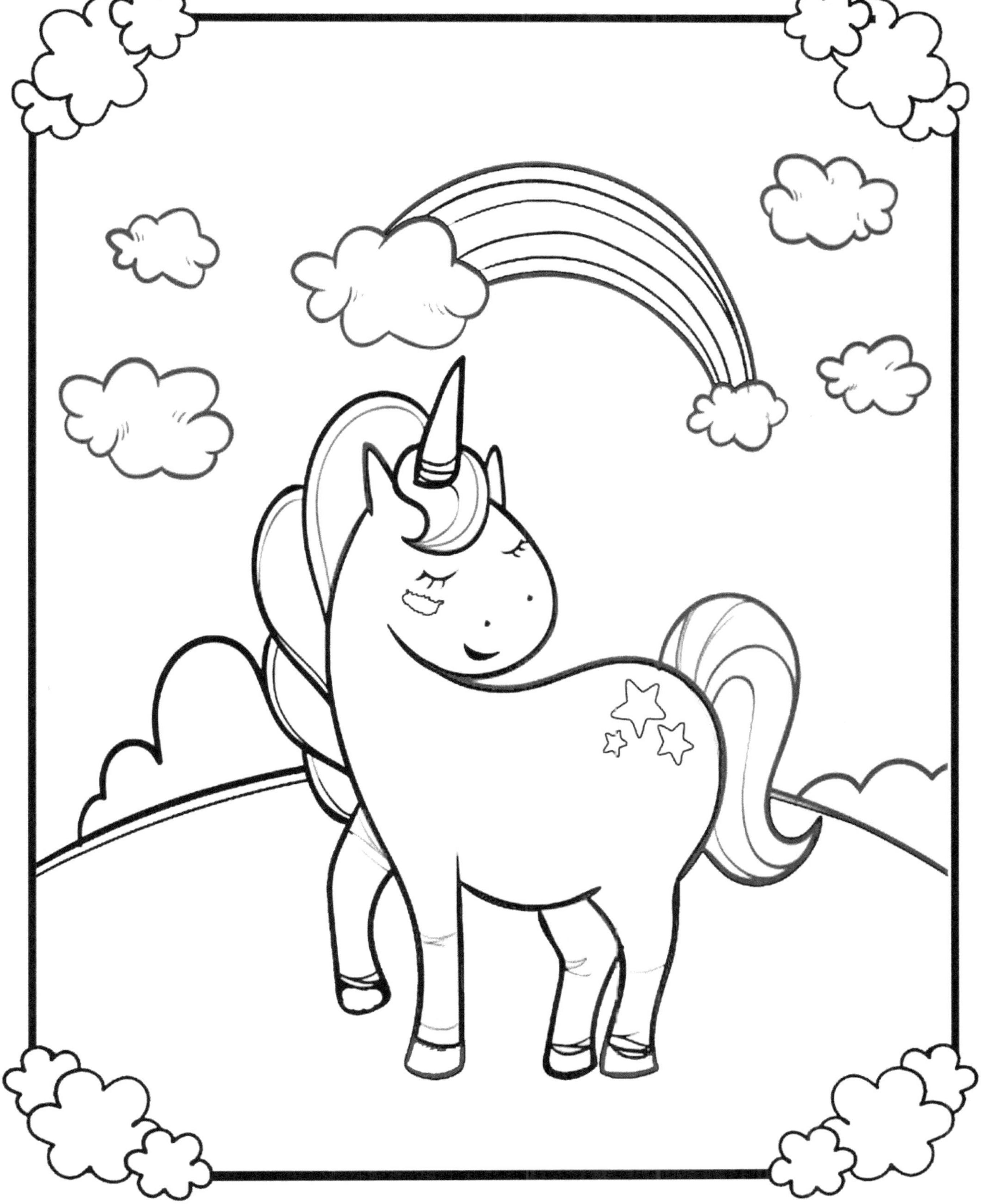

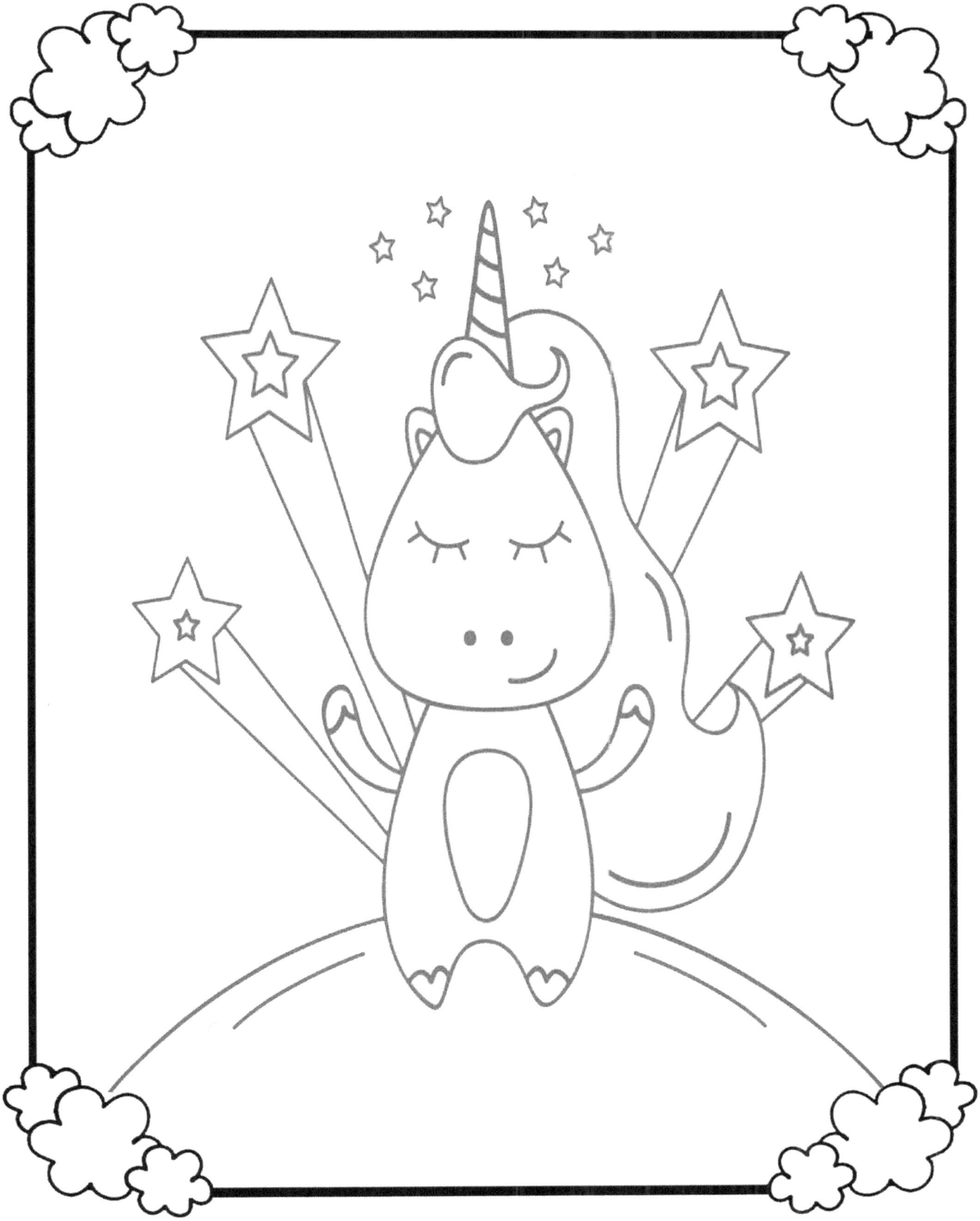

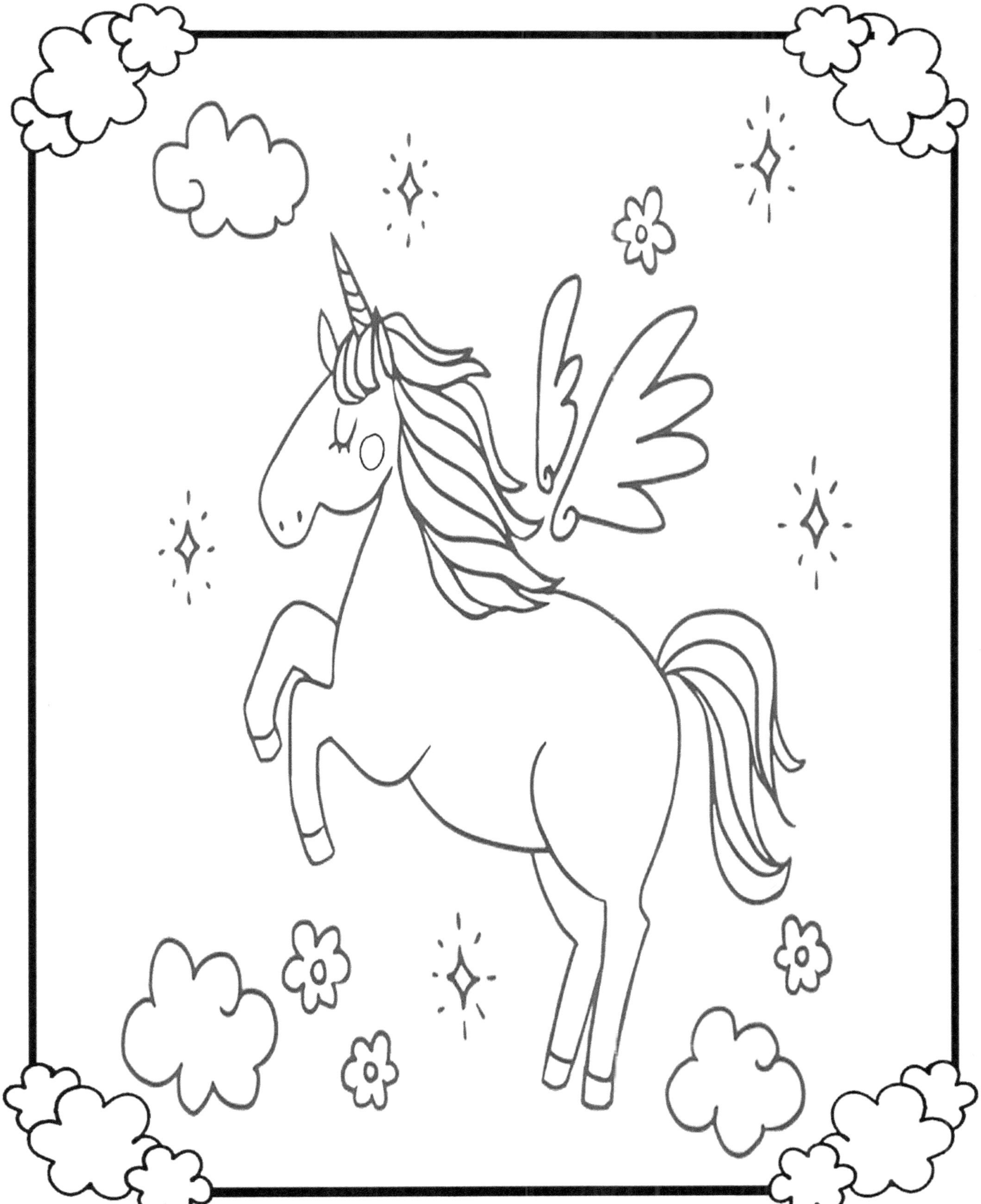

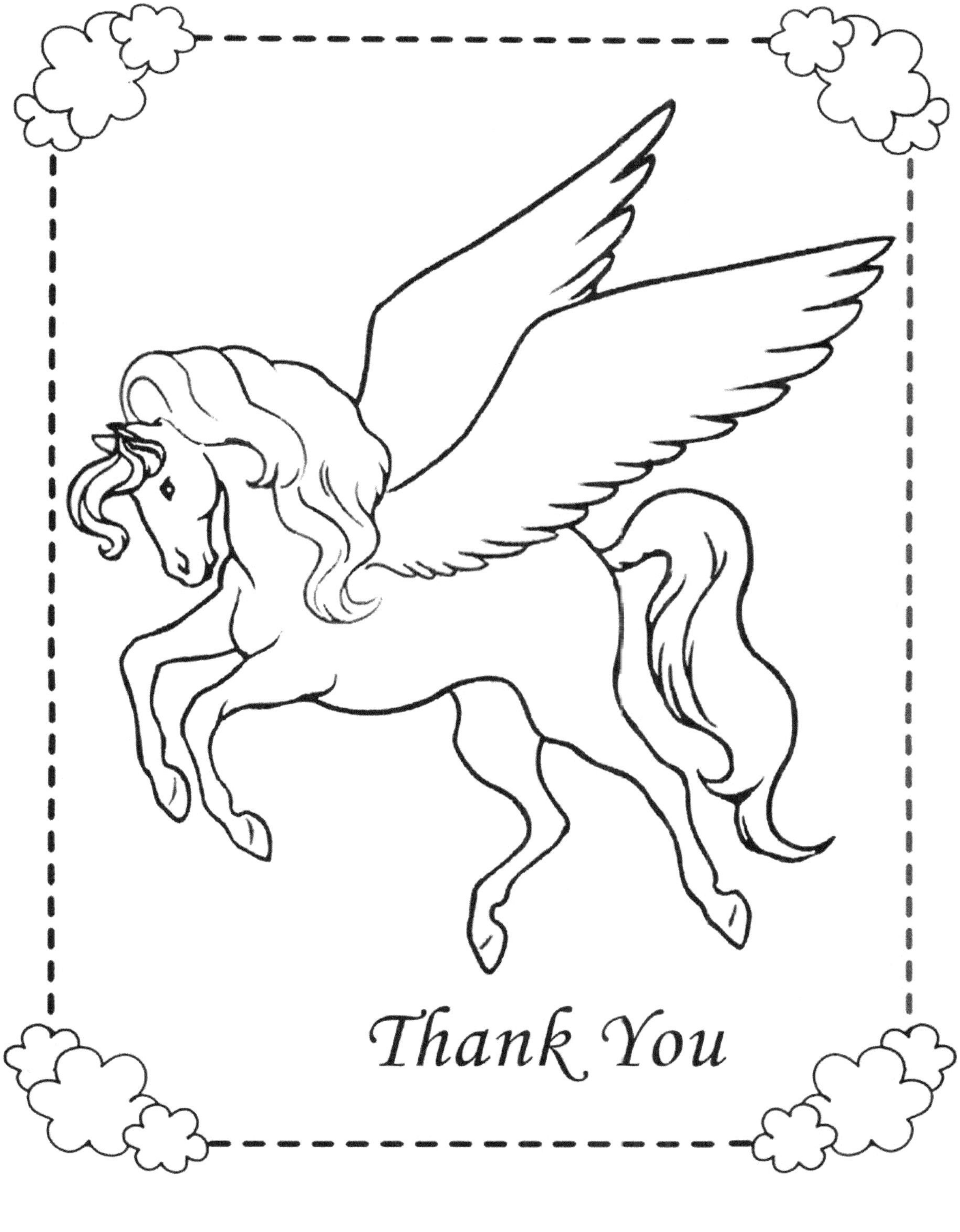
Thank You

www.ingramcontent.com/pod-product-compliance
Lightning Source LLC
Chambersburg PA
CBHW062123220526
45471CB00010B/3851